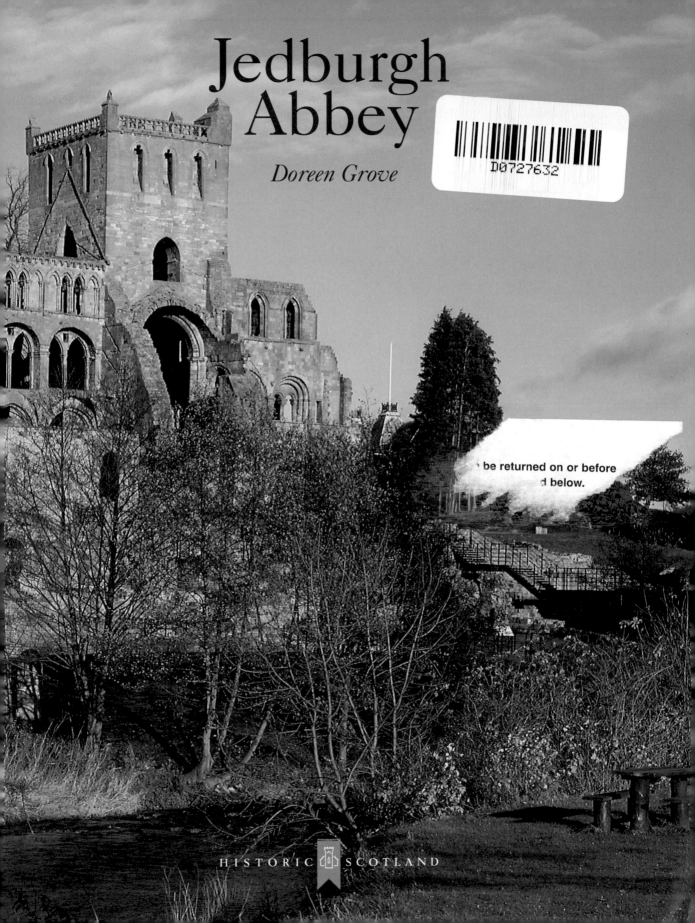

Jedburgh Abbey

Doreen Grove

HISTORIC SCOTLAND

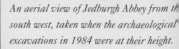

'The abbey was dedicated to the Virgin, and was amply endowed by David I and the nobles of the district.'

(David McGibbon and Thomas Ross, *The Ecclesiastical Architecture of Scotland*, 1896)

An aerial view of Jedburgh Abbey from the south west, taken when the archaeological excavations in 1984 were at their height.

A Guided Tour

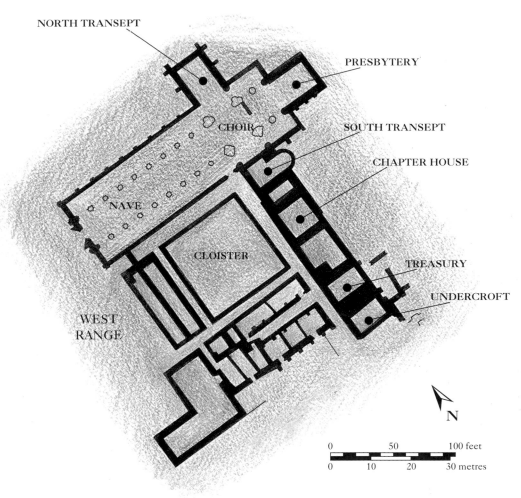

NORTH TRANSEPT

PRESBYTERY

SOUTH TRANSEPT

CHAPTER HOUSE

CHOIR

TREASURY

UNDERCROFT

NAVE

CLOISTER

WEST
RANGE

N

| 0 | | 50 | | 100 feet |
| 0 | 10 | 20 | | 30 metres |

This tour takes you through the ruins of the abbey, highlighting the architectural and archaeological features of interest. It begins in the visitor centre where an exhibition introduces the history of the abbey and displays some of the most beautiful objects found within it. The insight into life in medieval Scotland they offer is added to by a model of the abbey as it might have looked in 1500.

From the vantage point of the visitor centre a moment might be usefully spent contemplating the abbey. The church sits high above on the north of the site to ensure that it did not block light from the domestic ranges in front. Before building work could begin the natural river terraces had to be levelled to create platforms for the buildings around the cloister. Stone had to be quarried, probably from Ulston Moor, and carried the 2 km to the site. It is not surprising then that the abbey buildings took over 100 years to construct. First to be erected were temporary wooden structures providing basic accommodation for both canons and builders. The church, however, was the focus of the life of the canons and of early building work. It was followed by the construction of the east and south cloister ranges; and finally the west range was built to complete the cloister. The sloping site meant that the buildings on the south needed to be raised on a massively constructed undercroft to bring them level with the cloister. The first viewpoint is well placed to observe these works.

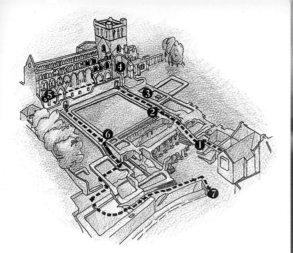

Viewpoint 1
Cellars of the East Range

The vaulted **undercroft** of the east range was built in the early thirteenth century. The dark, cool conditions made the cellars ideal for storage. Two floors above them was the canons' dormitory; at its south end was their toilet block, or reredorter. The reredorter emptied into a drain flushed by water channelled off the Jed Water.

The undercroft was abandoned a little over a century after it was built, probably because of war damage. The upper storeys seem to have been dealt a blow which caused a catastrophic failure of the building. A crude wall was built across part of the undercroft and the southern half was formed into a free-standing building. A **grain mill** eventually occupied this site, its mill-wheel driven by the water that had previously flushed the drains. The rest of the undercroft beyond the crude wall was abandoned and left to collect rubbish. The **mill-lade** continued to provide power until 1950 and still passes under the visitor centre.

The **vaulted chamber** north of the undercroft also has massively constructed north and south walls. Its small size and secure position may indicate that it was once the treasury.

The present cloister garden, laid out in 1986, with the impressive nave of the abbey church rising up behind.

The cellars at the south end of the east range during excavation in 1984, showing the quality of the thirteenth-century work. The two crude cross walls in the centre and the long wall (top right) date from a later period.

writing and contemplation. The **processional doors** between the church and the cloister can be seen at the north end of the east and west cloister walks. The east door is a fine example of the mason's craft of the 1180s; the west door is a reconstruction dated to 1876.

The twelfth-century cloister was extended to the south and west about the middle of the fourteenth century. Many of the domestic buildings were altered, perhaps making a virtue out of the necessity caused by battle-weary buildings.

The **east range** provided accommodation for the canons, where they had easy access to the church. The upper floor was occupied by their dormitory, a long room with the individual bed-spaces divided by curtains or timber partitions. At its north end would have been a night-stair into the south transept, making access for the early morning services easier. The position of this and the day-stair can no longer be traced (unless the latter lay within the thickened wall between the chapter house and warming house).

On the ground floor were several important rooms; close by the church was a vaulted passage, or **slype**, that led to the canons' burial-ground to the east. It probably also served as the parlour, where necessary conversation was permitted. Next to this was the chapter house (see viewpoint 3). Beyond was perhaps the **warming house**, or calefactory, where the canons were permitted to gather around the hearth on chilly winter days, but then only for short periods. Further south were the possible treasury and the storage cellars. This range was much altered during the life of the abbey and the upper part at least may have been abandoned in the sixteenth century as a result of war damage.

After the Reformation of 1560 the east range was demolished except for a vaulted passage, probably the slype, and three houses were built over it; one of these was later converted for use as a smithy. The southern end of the east range continued in light industrial use, mostly milling, long after the last canon died. The Jed Water provided power for a snuff mill, a little to the east of the abbey, as well as new woollen mills on the site of the old corn mill. The last of these closed down in the 1960s.

Viewpoint 2
The Cloister

The cloister was an open court that lay at the heart of the abbey. Around it ran the buildings that provided for almost all of the needs of the canons. In the centre of the cloister lay a **garden**. A covered **walkway** or cloister garth ran around its edge. This served as far more than a protected corridor connecting the important buildings of the abbey. The canons used it as a processional route during important services; and every day as a space for reading,

*The magnificent processional doorway
leading from the east cloister walk into
the east end of the church.*

Viewpoint 3
The Chapter House

The chapter house was the second most important building in the abbey after the church. It was the main meeting-place of the abbey; here the canons heard a chapter of their order each day. But it was also here that misdemeanours were confessed, punishments issued, instructions given and news broken. It is not surprising, therefore, to discover that the chapter house has a complex history.

Excavations in 1984 demonstrated that the original chapter house had sat unhappily with the east range, projecting just a short distance to the east, giving the impression that it was perhaps built first and the remainder of the range built around it. The first chapter house was not provided with stone seats, at least in the north, since burials were found right up to that wall. Later, this chapter house was extended to the east, presumably reflecting a growth in the size of the community. The larger chapter house is marked out by edge stones.

The east range (top) during the 1984 excavations, when the sequence of chapter houses was unravelled. The eastward extention of the chapter house is now marked out in stone strips (see page 9). X marks the spot where the Jedburgh Comb was found. The chapter house was a favoured place of burial as the lower illustration demonstrates.

The chapter house at Glenluce Abbey still stands entire and shows how the last chapter house at Jedburgh might have looked.

In the late fifteenth century, by which date the community had shrunk in size, the chapter house was reduced to the present square chamber, incorporated entirely within the east range, a development paralleled elsewhere in Scotland at Crossraguel, in Ayrshire, and Glenluce, in Galloway.

The chapter house was also an important burial-ground for officials of the abbey and generous benefactors. The 1984 excavations gave some insight into life and death in the abbey. When the burials were examined, although many of the bones were in poor condition, it was possible to spot cases of degenerative disease such as osteoarthritis and periostitis, as well as one possible sufferer from gout. Along with this came a catalogue of dental deterioration and at least one example of an abscess so severe it caused the deterioration of the bone around it. No doubt the medicinal herbs grown in the cloister garden for relieving pain were in great demand!

The Abbey Church

Like most major churches of the Middle Ages Jedburgh abbey church was laid out on a cross-shaped plan, with its head towards the east. At the east end lay the **presbytery**, containing the high altar. In front of this was the canons' **choir**, stretching below the tower and into the east end of the **nave**. The arms of the cross were formed by the **transepts** projecting on either side of the choir. The shaft of the cross formed the **nave**. The quality of the architecture and the unusually good survival here combine to make this church particularly worthy of study. The eastern end of the church provides an excellent comparison between the monumental strength of the Romanesque work of 1138 and the delicate Gothic of 40 years later.

The Romanesque east end of the church as it might have looked when first completed in the mid twelfth century.

Viewpoint 4
The East End

The church was the focus of life in the abbey; the prime purpose of the canons' lives was to dedicate themselves to God and to the teaching of his word. Several services were held before the high altar each day. The canons also had time for prayer and private dedication at additional altars. It was, therefore, important that the east end of the church was the first part of the abbey to be built and that it reflected these needs. The high altar was centrally placed at the very east end of the church in the presbytery. Extra altars were provided within the transepts and between the transepts and the presbytery, in the choir-aisle chapels. This created a stepped cross on plan. The original transepts had apsidal east ends and extended a single bay in width. The chapels and presbytery were both rectangular on plan.

There is evidence of at least three phases of development within the present east end. The 1138 church was built in the Romanesque style and can be best seen in the choir elevations. They have an unusual arrangement, with giant column-like piers with scalloped caps which rise through both the arcade and the gallery (there was originally no clearstorey or upper storey of windows). This work was clearly carried out by an experienced master-mason, who may have been brought to Jedburgh from either Tewkesbury, in Gloucestershire or Reading, in Berkshire. The design soon influenced other church buildings, most notably at Romsey Abbey, in Hampshire, built in the early 1100s. King David must have been familiar with Romsey. His aunt, Christina, was a nun there, and he attended his sister, Matilda, in the abbey when she was staying there before her marriage to Henry I (at a time when Romsey church was

The stout, strong piers on the north side of the choir are the earliest surviving part of the abbey church.

being planned). Jedburgh certainly owes more to Tewkesbury than Romsey. The original presbytery was shorter than the present layout. It probably had a lower storey consisting of an arcade of engaged arches, perhaps akin to those in the abbey church at Kelso. Above were round-topped windows. It was roofed over with a timber ceiling, probably a wagon vault. The first phase of building extended west to the first two bays of the nave, in order to provide a buttress for the bell tower over the crossing, as well as completing the space needed for the canons' choir.

The second phase began about 1180. The presbytery was rebuilt and extended; but there was no attempt to match the new architecture with the existing work. To light it new slender windows were set into an elegant arcade of alternate high and low pointed arches. A similar arrangement can be seen at Coldingham Priory, in Berwickshire. Below it was an arcade of engaged, decorated, pointed arches

One of the two-light upper openings through the south choir arcade.

The final phase of work was the building of a clearstorey, possibly in two phases. A low clearstorey was added to the east end of the church first. This was replaced with a taller clearstorey over the presbytery and choir (leaving the low clearstorey in the transepts). This was not completed until some time in the thirteenth century.

When finished, the choir and presbytery were enjoyed by the canons without disruption until the early fifteenth century. Rebuilding was perhaps prompted by the need to make good war damage, or there may have been a need to increase the number of altars. The first major works involved the reconstruction of the **north transept** to a larger rectangular plan. Its eastern wall was left blank to house elaborate altar-pieces, or retables, and the space was lit by large traceried windows in the north and west walls. It was probably built at the request of Bishop Turnbull of Glasgow (1447-54), who was also responsible for some alterations to the **chapel** on the south side of the choir; his coat-of-arms is emblazoned on one of the chapel buttresses. It is difficult to see what work was done in the chapel at this time because it was soon to be absorbed within a major reconstruction of the crossing area, necessitated as a result of the English attack of 1464, when the southern piers beneath the tower were rebuilt and strengthened. Following on from this the **tower** was reconstructed and a barrel vault added to the south transept. The heraldic devices of those who commissioned the work, Abbots John Hall (1478-84) and Thomas Cranston (1484-88), and Archbishop Robert Blackadder of Glasgow (1483-1508), can be found incorporated into the stonework.

The east end of the church as it might have looked in the early thirteenth century, after the modifications made to the presbytery and clearstorey.

The last of the medieval works visible at the east end demonstrate damage limitation on a tragic scale when the community was spiritually and financially exhausted. The crudely built walls and the lowered roofs were a desperate attempt to maintain a church in the crossing area. It is even possible that the community abandoned their dormitory in the east range of the cloister, and used the upper areas of the tower and transepts as safe accommodation after the attack of 1523. These works were only just complete when the attacks of 1544 and 1545 dealt the final blow. After that, the community seems only to have managed to block off and abandon the south transept in the hope that, in the future, they might find enough money to repair the damage. Alas, it was too late. The Reformation intervened and the truncated church in the crossing thereafter became the parish church. The north transept was adopted by the Ker family as their burial-aisle. It contains tombs and memorials from 1524, when Sir Andrew Ker of Fernieherst, Lord Warden of the Marches, was buried there, to the present day.

The piers supporting the bell tower, largely rebuilt following war damage in the mid-fifteenth century. Abbot Thomas Cranston's arms (inset) are visible on the furthest pier.

13

Viewpoint 5
The Nave

The nave was the only part of the abbey open to lay people. It is remarkable for its structural completeness, giving us an unparalleled impression of a medieval abbey church. Begun in the 1180s, it was not completed until early in the following century. It was planned on a grand scale; divided into nine bays flanked by an aisle on each side and three stories in height. The nave arcade has richly-moulded arches carried on eight lobed piers topped with elegant capitals. Above these the galleries have round-arched openings subdivided with two pointed arches in each bay and above them the clearstorey provided light for the nave with two windows in a continuous arcade of four arches to each bay. The appearance of the whole is light and airy, with the mass of stone being effortlessly supported, the very opposite of the strength and solidity found in the Romanesque elevations in the choir. The subtleties of the carving of the capitals and the forming of the vaults over the aisles show that the nave was probably built from west to east. It is worth venturing up the stairs in the west wall to look along the nave before going through the magnificent processional doorway in the west wall.

When the parish church within the crossing was declared dangerous in the late seventeenth century a new church was constructed in the five western bays of the nave. A gallery was inserted at the west end and access to it gained from the enlarged window in the south side of the west wall. The roof sprang from the top of the gallery and was entirely within the height of the earlier nave. The entrance to the church was through the west door and a door in the north wall which was provided with an external porch.

Jedburgh Abbey church from the north west. The rebuilt north transept is to the left of the lofty bell tower.

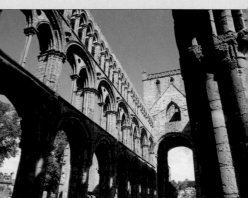

The nave from the east (above) and west (below).

The light, airy appearance of the upper
levels of the nave was achieved by an
extravagant array of decorated openings,
juxtaposing round-topped and pointed
arches effortlessly.

Through the west door is the magnificent **west front**. The elevation is so similar to Kelso Abbey that it is tempting to think that the masons may have worked there previously. The richly carved doorway is surmounted by three gablet niches which once held statues. The single tall window above was flanked by an elegant arcade and above is the gable, rebuilt in the fifteenth century, when the handsome rose window was inserted.

The magnificent west front and (inset) a detail of the entrance doorway.

Viewpoint 6
The West and South Ranges

The **west range** of the cloister housed accommodation requiring contact with the outside world. These would have included rooms for the cellarer, who was responsible for provisions, the almoner, who looked after the poor at the gate, and the guest master, who provided hospitality for travellers. Alas, nothing remains of this range except a large block of uncertain use at its southern end, adjacent to the canons' kitchen. After the Reformation, probably in the seventeenth century, the west range was rebuilt as a **manse** for the minister of the post-Reformation church. This remained on the site, with an increasing number of outbuildings, until 1876 when both church and manse were relocated to a new site over the Jed Water.

The canons' dining hall, or **refectory**, occupied the south side of the cloister. At some stage, perhaps after the English raids of the early fourteenth century, the canons decided to take advantage of a need to repair damage by extending the cloister to the west and south. This involved building a new west range and re-routing the south cloister walk through the range itself, while the refectory was relocated above the walkway and a narrow undercroft. Nothing remains of the refectory, but a drain which served the canons' washing place, or lavatory, can still be seen; the lavatory was always positioned near the entrance to the dining hall. At the west end of the dining hall are the remains of the **kitchens**.

Viewpoint 7
The West and South Ranges Beyond the Cloister

Beyond the cloister the **west range** continued with the small building already noted. This was incorporated into a larger building when the cloister was extended. It may have been part of a move to improve the western, public, approach to the abbey. The new building was provided with garderobes, or toilets, and was probably used for additional accommodation, perhaps a new guest-house.

To the south of the south range, between the dining hall and the river, is an **undercroft** of thirteenth-century date. It has been identified in the past with the infirmary, where sick and old monks followed a less harsh regime than in the dormitory and where the healthy brethren went regularly to be bled by leeches. Its position, however, is not where one would normally expect to find an infirmary; it was usually east of the cloister. The high quality of the architecture of the undercroft suggests that it may have formed part of the abbot's lodging. It was close enough to the canons' dormitory for him to be seen to be living communally with the canons but it was at a decent distance, as became his rank.

The merreles (nine-men's-morris) board, now on display in the visitor centre, was found during excavations in 1984 re-used as a building stone in the south range.

A finely carved statue of about 1180, now on display in the visitor centre. Statues such as these would have stood in the niches above the west door.

The Story of the Abbey

'The rule of the canons regular is the Rule of St Augustine, who drew his brethren to live together and tempered the rigour of his rule to their infirmity. Like a kind master, he did not drive his disciples with a rod of iron, but invited those who love the beauty of holiness to the door of salvation.'
(J W Clark, *The Observances in Use at the Augustinian Priory of St Giles and St Andrew at Barnwell*, 1897)

Jedburgh was founded as a priory by King David I and Bishop John of Glasgow no later than 1138. Their choice of site was far from arbitrary. Jedburgh had a long association with Christianity; indeed, a church has probably stood on this river haugh since the ninth century. But perhaps more importantly the king intended to use this dramatic site to demonstrate to Scots and English alike that he was able to build on a magnificent scale at the very fringe of the kingdom.

The community of Augustinian canons was to suffer many times for this brave show. Anglo-Scottish relations deteriorated after 1296 and the abbey became a front-line target. On numerous occasions the canons felt the rough hand of passing English armies. The final blow came in the 1540s when the devastation proved decisive and the abbey never properly recovered. The Reformation in 1560 saw the final decline. The church alone survived because of its continued use by the parishioners right up to 1875, leaving us the magnificent legacy of a roofless, but otherwise almost complete, twelfth- and early thirteenth-century church.

The Early Church

A ninth- or tenth-century crude carved stone depicting on the upper face Christ in His Majesty above tormented souls with other figure-work down the sides. The stone was found in 1984 re-used as a building block in the medieval abbey.

When Bishop Ecgred of Lindisfarne built a church at Gedwearde (Jedworth) in 830 he may have been establishing a church at a site already known for its Christian associations. One of the finest shrine fragments in Scotland comes from in or near Jedburgh and is dated to the early eighth century (see page 21).

A shrine of this quality could only have been created for someone of great wealth or sanctity and must surely have been erected inside or alongside a church. In addition to the shrine, several other fragments of Early Christian stones and several Anglo-Saxon coins have been found in Jedburgh. It is not possible to trace the church built by Ecgred, a hunt further complicated because he founded two settlements within a few miles of each other, both called Jedworth.

In 1080 a church does emerge from the shadows in a most melodramatic way. In that year Bishop Walcher of Durham was assassinated. The leader of the killers, Eadwulf Rus, grandson of Earl Uchtred of Northumbria, fled to Jedburgh. Shortly afterwards Rus himself was killed, by a woman, and buried in the church at 'Geddewerde'. Later, his body was exhumed and thrown out of the church 'as if it were filth' by Turgot, Archdeacon of Durham. This must have been at some time before 1107, when Turgot became Bishop of St Andrews.

The Jedburgh Comb

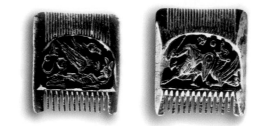

It is very tempting to associate the story of Eadwulf Rus with a discovery made during excavation in 1984, when the upper torso of a man was discovered. It had been thrown into a sewage ditch just eastward of the chapter house (see page 7). Along with it were found a magnificent ivory comb, dated to about 1100, and other objects, undoubtedly fitting belongings for the grandson of an earl. Unfortunately, the facts do not quite measure up to a modern criminal investigation. The part-torso was still articulated and must, therefore, have been thrown into the ditch soon after death; however, the associated objects cannot be pinned down in date closely enough to support a 1080s' date. It may not be Eadwulf Rus, but whoever he was, he was almost certainly murdered. But what was the motive? A case for Brother Cadfael, perhaps?

lamp

cooking pot

seal matrix (left) and buckle (right) with whetstone

*Part of the splendid eighth-century shrine, decorated
with vine scroll inhabited by birds and beasts.
A work of this quality must have been designed to
hold the body of someone greatly revered.*

21

The Augustinian Foundation

J edburgh Priory was founded shortly after Bishop John's return to Scotland in 1137 from two years spent at the Benedictine house of Tiron, near Chartres. The founding brethren, though, were probably brought from St Quentin Abbey, at Beauvais. David I and Bishop John were both genuinely pious and lived at a time when the Church in Europe was undergoing a renaissance. Under their influence the Scottish Church embarked on its own renewal. Both men also appreciated the political as well as the spiritual advantage of a strong Church. David in particular had spent his youth at the court of his brother-in-law, Henry I of England, where he observed not only the magnificence of the great church buildings, but also how well they played their part alongside the royal castles in governing the local population.

During his years abroad, David became familiar with the blossoming new religious orders spreading across Europe. Jedburgh provided a perfect spot for a new royal foundation in several ways. It was David's aim to reorganise the Church in Scotland and, in doing so, to loosen the grip of the Archbishop of York who claimed authority over it, a struggle he shared with Bishop John. At Jedburgh, David was able to demonstrate that he was in a position to build on a grand scale, on the very border with England.

The king was not alone in the generous endowments he granted to the new priory; several great landowners were similarly persuaded. Chief among them was Ranulf de Soules, the king's butler and Lord of Liddesdale, who donated the church of St Martin, close by his castle at Liddel, together with the teind of all his venison in Liddesdale.

The priory had English benefactors too, including William de Vieuxpont of Westmoreland. Some not only gave land but donated parish churches; Jedburgh eventually possessed about 20 such churches. The canons not only took the income from the churches but controlled the preaching within them.

Before 1154 Jedburgh's status was raised to that of an abbey, and it increased in wealth and authority. Eventually it came to have the priories of Blantyre, in Lanarkshire, Canonbie, in Dumfriesshire, and Restenneth, in Angus, dependent upon it.

Restenneth Priory, near Forfar, founded as a daughter house of Jedburgh about 1140. The priory ruins are also in Historic Scotland's care.

The Augustinian Order

The brethren at Jedburgh were part of an order of canons which took its title from St Augustine of Hippo, who died in AD 430. Like many religious groups in the eleventh century, priests sought out the teachings of a saint who could provide spiritual guidance for the foundation of a distinct order. The Augustinian Order was recognised in 1059.

The Augustinians, or 'black canons' as they were known by the colour of their habit, were not monks but priests who lived a cloistered and contemplative life. Their regime was less rigorous, their services were shorter and they were not entirely cut off from the outside world.

The brothers would often leave the abbey to preach in their parishes. Nonetheless, their lives were essentially monastic, for they were bound by the vows of poverty, chastity and obedience and their reason for retiring from the world was the same, to dedicate their lives to God. This meant that most of their days were spent in the cloister, attending the daily round of services of psalms, prayers and anthems, starting in the early hours of the morning and finishing in the early evening. Although their church services were probably shorter than those of the monks, worship still dominated their lives. Between these services were others, including one or more Mass in the lay section of the church; there was also time for spiritual, intellectual or even manual activity. The gardens had to be tended, services and new books written, meals made and guests looked after. Patients in the infirmary had to be cared for and the daily meeting in the chapter house had to be attended.

An Augustinian (black) canon dressed in his habit (from Dugdale's Monasticon Anglicanum, *1655-73).*

The abbey as it might have look about 1200 when building work would have been at its height. Throughout the 400-year existence of the abbey, the canons would rarely have been without the ringing sound of chisel and mell.

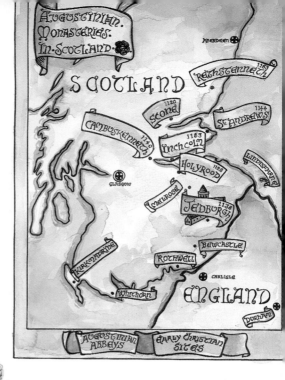

It is not clear why David chose the Augustinian Order for Jedburgh. He had a comprehensive knowledge of most of the religious orders that were emerging during this time of fervent religious renewal. Indeed, he was responsible for the introduction of the very first reformed monastic house in Britain when he founded a house for the Tironensian Order at Selkirk in 1113 (it was later moved to Kelso). He also established the greatest of the reformed orders, the Cistercians, at Melrose in 1136. It may be significant that the Augustinian houses were located close to the seats of government, like Holyrood, beside Edinburgh Castle, and Cambuskenneth, near Stirling. The order was also established at the symbolically important site of Scone, the ancient seat of Scottish kings, and at the cathedral church of St Andrews; the premier church in Scotland in the Middle Ages. Their abbots and priors were important political figures, frequently found at the royal court. The royal castle in Jedburgh was often visited by the royal court and it was on one such visit that Malcolm IV, David's grandson, died in 1165.

The Abbey and the Town

By the thirteenth century Jedburgh was booming. The royal castle had been long established as a favoured residence of the court, the abbey was rich and influential, and the royal burgh, first given a charter in 1170, was flourishing.

CASTLE
(Dismantled in 1409)

TOWNHEAD PORT

TOWNHEAD

SKIPRUNNING BURN

LAWNMARKET

DABIE'S TOWER

ABBEY PRECINCT

ABBEY

ST. N
TOW

JED WATER

The site of Jedburgh Castle is now occupied by an early town jail, built in 1823 and now serving as a local museum.

The burgh had developed in a cruciform plan with the main street running northward from the castle to a ford across the Jed Water leading to Bongate. The east-west road ran from another ford (close to the existing late-medieval Canongate Bridge), along Canongate and through the market-place to a point on Burn Wynd where the road crossed the Skiprunning Burn. That burn and the Jed Water together formed the boundaries of the burgage plots and probably defined the town. Each entrance point into the town was protected by a strong port, or gate, which served both to regulate trade and to defend the town. They were in addition to those gates protecting the entrances into the abbey precinct itself, which probably occupied all of the land within the sweep of the Jed Water from Abbey Close to Canongate.

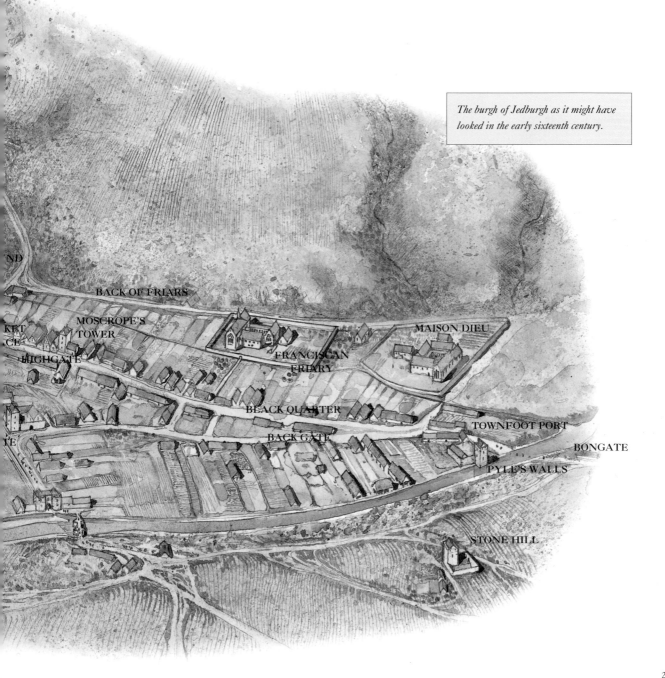

The burgh of Jedburgh as it might have looked in the early sixteenth century.

A Wedding and Two Funerals

In 1285, Alexander III, married his second queen, Yolande de Dreux, in the abbey at Jedburgh. The church was magnificently decorated and thronging with guests when, legend tells us, a ghostly figure appeared before the congregation and foretold the king's death. Alexander did die in the following year. It was that death, followed by the sad death of his young granddaughter and heir, Margaret, the Maid of Norway, in 1290, and the short, ill-starred reign of John Balliol (1292-96) that formed the prelude to the long and bloody Wars of Independence with England.

A stained-glass window in Lerwick Town Hall, Shetland, depicting Margaret 'the Maid of Norway'.

King Alexander III sits at the right hand of the English king, Edward I, at a meeting of the English parliament. Llywelyn, Prince of Wales, sits on King Edward's other side; from the sixteenth-century Wriothesley Manuscript. (Courtesy of The Royal Collection, © Her Majesty the Queen).

The Abbey at War

Jedburgh was plunged into the conflict soon after the outbreak of hostilities when, in 1296, Edward I of England lodged in the abbey. During his stay he contrived the election of a pro-English abbot, but this did not save the brethren from the ravages of the fighting, from both sides. In 1305 the lead was stripped from the roofs by English troops under Sir Richard Hastings' command, not necessarily an entirely spiteful act for lead was needed to make siege engines. Throughout the war the canons walked a political tightrope. Despite Hastings' attack (or perhaps because of it), their leanings seem to have been towards the English and in 1307 Edward II wrote to Abbot William entreating him to keep the peace. The abbey was clearly thought to offer its support to the English cause. But by 1312 life had become intolerable for the community for the Scots had recaptured Roxburgh Castle, beside Kelso, and were threatening Jedburgh, leaving the canons feeling vulnerable. The abbot and 11 canons fled across the Border to take refuge on their lands in Yorkshire. For the next decade at least some of the community remained in exile. Only through the massive spiritual effort of Abbot Kennock, who it is said maintained peace for that decade through the sheer power of prayer, did the canons survive their ordeal.

The upper part of the bell tower shows evidence of regular rebuilding.

The tranquil spot chosen by King David I to show he could build close to the English Border proved to be a major inconvenience for future generations of canons; Jedburgh was the first target for every English army crossing this part of the Border.

During the later fourteenth century the community, along with the nation, rebuilt its buildings and its wealth. The cloister was enlarged; so too was the chapter house. It is safe to assume, therefore, that the community grew with them. In the fifteenth century, however, Jedburgh was again under fire. There were damaging attacks in 1409, when Jedburgh Castle was destroyed, and in 1410, 1416 and 1464. These attacks were costly on the welfare of both the canons and their buildings. Recruiting novices must have been increasingly difficult for a house that was so regularly in the path of an army.

When efforts were made to unite Restenneth Priory with Jedburgh in 1476 the monastic buildings were said to be in need of repair. By 1502 the situation had worsened. Reports of this nature were often exaggerated, in order to attract financial help. However, in Jedburgh's case, the church itself provides ample evidence of the major work undertaken by successive abbots between 1464 and 1520, particularly in the area of the crossing.

In 1523 the Earl of Surrey's army attacked and burned the abbey. The devastation wrought must have been immense for the community was driven to desperate measures. Within the church, roofs were lowered, and roughly built walls were inserted to restrict the church to an area below the crossing-tower. It is possible that at least some of the domestic accommodation was too badly damaged to continue in use.

The works in the church can only just have been completed when, in 1544, the Earl of Hertford was sent north with an army by Henry VIII of England.

Their task was to persuade the Scots of the merit of a marriage between the infant Queen Mary and her half cousin, Henry's son, Prince Edward, the future Edward VI of England. To add insult to injury, a letter from Hertford to his king describing Jedburgh as 'a house of some strength, and may be made a good fortress' would surely have sent a shiver down the spines of the canons. It is unlikely that the abbey was fortified in that year or the following one, when Hertford returned. But those two serious attacks left the abbey so badly damaged that it seems the idea was taken up later in the decade. The English certainly occupied Jedburgh after their unexpected success at the Battle of Pinkie, near Musselburgh, in 1547, but from the spring of the following year a French force, of some 1500 men and 500 horse, under the command of General D'Esse, held the town. Since Jedburgh no longer had a castle and the only protection was the abbey precinct wall with its gate towers, the French decided to fortify at least part of the abbey itself. This involved levelling some of the badly damaged buildings to create gun-platforms and building an earthwork, named 'the Ramparts' by the nineteenth century, to protect the east flank of the abbey.

The abbey as it might have looked in 1548, by which date much of the fabric was sadly dilapidated, chiefly through the ravages of war. By now the canons were residing in the safety of the bell tower, while another sort of cannon may well have bristled from hastily built emplacements in and around the abbey complex. In 1548, General D'Esse and his sizeable French force are known to have fortified this part of the town.

The Final Chapter

It is perhaps ironic that the emergency work undertaken by the monks to maintain a church in the crossing also enabled it to survive as the parish church after the Reformation. But who was left in 1560? It is unlikely that any more than eight canons were still in residence, and these would have been permitted to live out the rest of their days in the crumbling abbey so long as they embraced the reformed religion.

Since the abbey church at Jedburgh had served the local parishioners as well as the canons from at least the early thirteenth century, it continued to be used for worship after the Reformation. It seems likely, however, that only part of the area beneath the central tower and transepts was fully usable, and it was in this area that a new parish church was formed. By 1574 the roof of even this part was in advanced decay and it was proposed to repair it using the roof over the old refectory. There were further problems in 1636 when one of the piers holding up the tower was judged to be at risk. In 1642 John Myln, the royal master-mason, was asked to give his advice on the problem. Little was done to act on his recommendations, fortunately for us since they included substantial demolition. In the event, between 1668 and 1671 a new church was created in the western part of the nave.

In 1681 much of the north transept was walled off by the Ker family, the ancestors of the Marquises of Lothian, who had long used it as their burial-place. The cloister buildings were used as quarries for stone. A manse and stables was built over the west range and three houses on the ruins of the east range; one was later converted into a smithy. More mills, including a textile mill, were built at the south-east corner of the cloister and operated until the 1960s.

The major turning-point in the abbey's modern history was the decision in 1875 to build a new parish church over the Jed Water, largely at the behest of the ninth Marquis of Lothian. He subsequently paid for major repairs to the ancient fabric, and in 1913 the ruin was the first of the great Border abbeys to pass into State care.

The ruined abbey from the Jed Water in 1793, with the wester[n] part of the nave still in use as t[he] parish kirk (note the glazing in the gallery arches). The gabled building in the foreground was the manse, sitting on the site of [the] west range, while over on the ea[st] range new houses had been buil[t]. Left: the Ker family's armorial, dated 1681, situated above the door into their burial aisle in t[he] north transept.

An eighteenth-century view of the ruined church from the north east showing the later parish kirk within the western part of the nave.

The splendid west front of the abbey church from Abbey Close about 1870; the parish kirk doors are still in place.

The choir of Jedburgh Old Parish Church pose before the restored west processional doorway about 1880.

The Cloister Garden

'The garden should be ornamented with roses and lilies, the heliotrope, violets and mandrakes. There should be made beds for onions, leeks, garlic, pumpkins and shallots. . . There should not be lacking pot vegetables.'
(Alexander Neckham (*c.* 1215), Augustinian canon and author of *De Naturis Rerum*, 'Concerning the Nature of Things')

Throughout the Middle Ages, religious houses led the way in nurturing varieties of fruits and vegetables, in developing gardening skills and the commercial supply of seeds and plants, and in advancing medical science through the careful application of herbal remedies. The Augustinians made a leading contribution.

Jedburgh Abbey was no exception and all available open space within the sprawling precinct, including the cloister court, would have been put to good, practical use as garden ground and orchard. The brethren were self-sufficient in most things, growing flowers for the altars in the church, vegetables, fruit and pot herbs for the refectory table, medicinal herbs for the infirmary and a miscellany of other plants for a variety of uses.

No records survive to show how the cloister may have looked during the abbey's existence, and archaeological excavations in 1984 shed little light on this aspect of monastery life. The present cloister garden, planted in 1986, is designed to give an impression of how a typical Scottish monastery garden may have looked about 1500. Fruit trees and bushes planted elsewhere in the abbey grounds give a further flavour of the richness of garden produce available to the brethren throughout the 400-year existence of the abbey.

The square, gravelled **court** defined by **yew hedging** echoes the extent of the first cloister laid out in the early twelfth century. A **juniper** serves as the central feature from which radiate

beds containing **plants from early times**. The **grassy fringe** to the west and south of the gravelled court reflects the enlargement of the cloister court in the fourteenth century. This 'flowery mede' has raised beds laid out formally in the style then fashionable and growing **pot herbs and medicinal herbs** of the time together with **plants for a purpose**.

The court within the yew hedge is planted with early varieties of plants which had many uses; indeed, the **yew** itself, which could bear heavy weights of snow, was used as a protective cover and came to symbolise immortality. At the centre of the garden is another symbolic tree, the **juniper**, which represented the Tree of Life. Yet it too had practical uses. Its branches were used to sprinkle holy water, its oil was used to treat sheep-scab, its wood was good for smoking fish and its heartwood valued for wood carving, its bark could be made into rope and its roots woven into baskets, and the berries were prized in cooking. In the five radiating **flower beds** are flowers and plants that would have been well known to the early canons, including damask rose, hyssop, alkanet and cotton lavender.

The **raised beds** among the 'flowery mede' contain a variety of plants usable in diverse ways. The likes of the acanthus, fern and columbine made excellent altar decorations, whilst others were used also in tonics, for a variety of culinary uses, and to provide soothing balms and more painful purgatives. Catkins from the pussy willow were used to stuff pillows and ivy made baskets and hay-forks. Perhaps the most versatile was the common elder. Its flowers were used for cordials, its berries for wine and jelly. Fevers, coughs and eye irritations were treated by lotions made from its flowers, a healing ointment was made from its leaves, the corky bark made a purgative, and an infusion of the leaves gave an insect repellant.

But the cloister garden was also valued as a refuge from the hustle and bustle of the abbey. Quiet contemplation amid the scented flowers, humming to the sound of bees and gently wafting in the summer breeze, must have made it as much a pleasure then as it is today.

...he cloister garden is laid out with some of the ...owers and herbs that might have delighted the ...nses of the canons and provided them with ...od, herbs and medicines.

Broom, hyssop, damask rose and rosemary all produced flowers to decorate the church, but like most plants in the canons' garden each had other uses, from basket making to the preparation of medicines.

FURTHER READING

For further information about the history and architecture of Jedburgh Abbey, the following are recommended:

J Watson
Jedburgh Abbey and the Abbeys of Teviotdale (1894)

Royal Commission on the Ancient and Historical Monuments of Scotland *Roxburghshire Inventory*, vol. 2 (1956)

I Cowan and D Easson
Medieval Religious Houses: Scotland (1976)

T Garton
'The transitional sculpture of Jedburgh Abbey', in *Romanesque and Gothic: essays for George Zarnecki* (1987)

J Lewis and G Ewart
Jedburgh Abbey: the archaeology and architecture of a Border abbey (1995)

M Thurlby
'Jedburgh Abbey Church: the Romanesque fabric', *Proceedings of the Society of Antiquaries of Scotland*, 125 (1995)

J Reid
The Scots Gardner (1683; reprinted 1988)

J Harvey
Medieval Gardens (1981)

N Culpepper
Complete Herbal and English Physician (1826; reprinted 1981)